MAGIC

Mermaids

ASTRID EBONYWOOD

Contents Page

$\mathcal{G}$reetings,

Welcome to "Magical Mermaids: Using the Essence of Mermaid Power to Enhance Your Witchcraft and Spiritual Practice". This book is a comprehensive guide to the world of mermaid energy and magic, designed to help you tap into the power of these amazing creatures and enhance your spiritual practice. Whether you're a current practitioner or just starting out on your magical journey, this book is full of practical techniques, tips, and exercises to help you connect with the essence of mermaids and harness their power for your own growth and transformation.

From the history and mythology of mermaids to the techniques for spells, meditations, and energy work, this book will take you on a journey through the world of mermaid magic and show you how to incorporate it into your daily life. Whether you're looking to heal your body and soul, protect yourself from negativity, or bring your manifestation goals to life, this book has everything you need to dive into the world of mermaid magic and unleash your inner power.

So, get ready to embrace the magic of the merfolk and let their essence enhance your spiritual practice.

With "Magical Mermaids", you'll discover the power and magic that lies within, and learn how to harness it to create the life you've always dreamed of.

So, let's begin this aquatic adventure together, and may the magic within you always shine brightly.

Brightest Blessings

I. Introduction

A. Definition of Mermaids

 A mermaid is a mythical aquatic creature that is half-human and half-fish.

Mermaids are often depicted with a female human upper body and a fishtail below the waist. They are often associated with the sea, oceans, and marine life and are seen as powerful beings with magical abilities.

In many cultures, mermaids are revered as symbols of beauty, grace, and mystery.

In folklore, mermaids have been depicted as powerful sirens who lure sailors to their death, as well as helpful and benevolent creatures who aid those in need.

The concept of mermaids has been popular for thousands of years and continues to captivate the imagination of people around the world.

B. Mermaids in Mythology and Folklore

Mermaids have been part of human mythology and folklore for thousands of years and can be found in cultures all over the world.

In ancient Greek mythology, the most famous mermaid was the sea nymph Thetis, who was said to have the power to calm the seas and create storms.

As for Norse mythology, the mermaid-like being named Ran was said to rule over the underwater kingdom and have control over the tides.

European folklore tells of mermaids who were often depicted as dangerous creatures who lured sailors to their death with their enchanting songs.

In contrast, in African folklore, mermaids were often seen as wise and powerful beings who protected the waters and the creatures that lived within them.

And in some Native American cultures, mermaids were revered as spiritual beings who possessed healing powers and could bring good luck.

In popular culture, mermaids have been depicted in many forms, from animated films and TV shows to literature and art. The story of The Little Mermaid, written by Hans Christian Andersen, is one of the most well-known tales and has been adapted into various forms of media. Mermaids continue to capture the imagination of people and their popularity continues to grow.

The overall concept of mermaids has a rich history in mythology and folklore and continues to be an important part of our cultural heritage. Their versatile and enduring nature has made them an enduring symbol of mystery, beauty, and power.

C. The Concept of Mermaid Power

The concept of mermaid power refers to the mystical energy or essence associated with mermaids that is believed to have magical properties. This power is said to be associated with the ocean and its inhabitants, as well as with the qualities commonly attributed to mermaids, such as beauty, grace, and mystery.

In many cultures, mermaids are seen as powerful beings with the ability to control the oceans, the weather, and even the lives of humans. Their songs were said to have the power to entice and enchant those who heard them, while their tears were said to possess healing powers. In many myths and legends, mermaids are seen as protectors of the oceans and the creatures that live within them.

In the context of spiritual and magical practices, mermaid power is often invoked and harnessed to enhance spell work, promote physical and mental wellbeing, and increase personal strength and insight. Some practitioners believe that connecting with the essence of merfolk can help them tap into the magic of the ocean and the wisdom of the underwater realm. Others believe that mermaids can help them connect with their intuition, creativity, and emotions, and bring balance to their lives.

In conclusion, the idea of utilising the power of mermaids is a deeply ingrained part of human mystery and continues to play an important role in spiritual and magical practices. The idea of harnessing the energy and essence of mermaids to enhance one's life is an intriguing and popular concept that has inspired countless people over the ages.

D. Purpose of the Book

The purpose of the book "Magical Mermaids: Using the Essence of Mermaids Power to Enhance Your Witchcraft and Spiritual Practice" is to explore the world of mermaids and their associated energy and provide practical guidance for using this energy for personal growth and spiritual development.

The book aims to provide you with a comprehensive understanding of mermaids and their spirit, and how their energy can be incorporated into witchcraft and spiritual crafts. It will cover various techniques for connecting with merfolk, using their essence in spell work and much more, and offer you the opportunity to explore advanced topics such as dream magic and manifestation.

The book is intended to be an accessible and practical guide for you if you are interested in mer-magic, whether you are a beginner or an experienced practitioner. The book will provide you with an in-depth understanding of the concept, as well as practical tools and techniques for invoking this energy into your own life.

Overall, the book will help you tap into the immense power of merfolk and enhance your craft in meaningful and effective ways. If you are looking to improve their spiritual connection, increase your personal power, or simply learn more about the fascinating world of mermaids, this book will provide valuable insights and guidance.

II. Understanding Mermaid Energy

A. Characteristics of Mermaid Energy

Mermaid energy refers to the energy or essence associated with mermaids that is believed to have magical properties. Understanding this energy is key to being able to effectively incorporate it into your life in any way you wish.

This sort of energy is associated with the ocean and its inhabitants, as well as the qualities commonly attributed to mermaids This energy is believed to be fluid, graceful, and intuitive, and to have a powerful influence on the emotions, creativity, and intuition.

In many cultures, mermaids are seen as powerful beings with the ability to control the seas, the weather, and even the lives of humans. Their songs were said to have the power to entice and enchant those who heard them, while their tears were said to possess healing powers. In many myths and legends, mermaids take on the role of the protector, a reason that makes their energy so appealing to those in times of great need.

To connect with mermaid energy, it is important to understand its associated qualities and to cultivate these qualities within yourself. This might involve meditating on the ocean, near water or in the presence of its inhabitants. Practicing water-based rituals, or incorporating ocean-themed imagery into your spell work can also help with this.

It is also important to develop an intuitive connection with the energy of merfolk. This can be done through visualisation, affirmations, or dream work. By connecting with the their spirit in this way, you can tap into its qualities and incorporate them into your magical work in meaningful ways.

Understanding mermaid energy is essential to using it wisely in your craft. By developing a deeper connection with this energy, you can enhance your personal power, improve your ethereal energies, and tap into the magic of the ocean and the wisdom of the underwater realm.

The characteristics of mermaid energy are believed to include:

Fluidity: Mermaid energy is often described as fluid, graceful, and flowing, reflecting the movements of the ocean and its inhabitants.

Intuition: Mermaids are often associated with intuition and emotional intelligence, and their energy is believed to enhance these qualities in those who connect with it.

Creativity: Mermaids are often seen as creatures of beauty and grace, and their energy is believed to stimulate creativity and imagination.

Mystery: Mermaids are mysterious beings, associated with the unknown depths of the ocean. Their energy is believed to embody this sense of mystery and the unknown.

Empathy: Mermaids are often seen as protectors of the oceans and its inhabitants, and their energy is believed to enhance empathy and compassion.

Healing: Mermaids are often associated with healing, both physical, menta, emotional and spiritual, and their energy is believed to have a therapeutic effect on those who connect with it.

Connection: Mermaids are seen as symbols of the ocean and its interconnectedness, and their energy is believed to promote a deeper connection with the natural world and with one's own intuition and emotions.

By understanding and cultivating these characteristics, practitioners can tap into the power of mermaid energy and incorporate it into their witchcraft and spiritual practice. Whether they are seeking to improve their spiritual connection, increase their personal power, or simply explore the magic of the ocean realm, mermaid energy provides a rich source of inspiration and guidance.

B. How to Connect with Mermaid Energy

There are several ways to connect with mermaid energy and incorporate it into your witchcraft and spiritual practice. Some methods include:

Meditations: Meditation is a powerful tool for connecting with mermaid energy. You can visualise yourself swimming in the ocean, surrounded by its beauty and grace, or imagine yourself as a mermaid, with the ability to control the ocean and its inhabitants.

Water-based rituals: Performing water-based rituals can help you connect with the energy. This might involve performing a ritual bath or shower or submerging yourself in a body of water while focusing on your intention to connect with mermaids.

Ocean-themed imagery: Incorporating ocean-themed imagery into your spell work or altar can help you connect with mermaid energy. This might include using seashells, ocean-themed candles, or mermaid figurines.

Affirmations: Affirmations are a powerful tool for connecting with mermaid energy. You can use affirmations to focus your intention and cultivate the qualities associated with mermaids, such as fluidity, intuition, creativity, and empathy.

Dream work: Mermaids are often associated with the dream realm, and incorporating mermaid imagery or themes into your dream work can help you connect with their energy. This might involve keeping a dream journal, meditating on mermaids before bed, or working with mermaid tarot cards.

Music: Listening to music that evokes the ocean, and its inhabitants can help you connect with mermaid energy. This might include ocean-themed music, or songs that feature the sounds of waves, seagulls, or other ocean creatures.

By adding these methods into your practice, you can create a deeper connection with merfolk and tap into their amazing magic. By working on these techniques, you can you achieve your goals.

C. Invoking the Spirit of Mermaids

Invoking the spirit of mermaids is a powerful tool to connect with them and adding it into your witchcraft. Here is a simple ritual you can perform to invoke the spirit of mermaids:

1. Find a quiet, peaceful place where you will not be disturbed. You may choose to set up an altar with ocean-themed items such as seashells, ocean-themed candles, or mermaid figurines.

2. Cleanse your energy by taking a bath or shower, smudging yourself with sage, or performing any other energy-clearing technique that resonates with you.

3. Stand facing the ocean or a body of water and call upon the spirits of the ocean to witness your ritual. You may use a ritual chant or prayer, or simply speak from your heart. For example: -

   "Mermaids of the underwater realm, I call upon the presence of your light and love to guide me on my path."

4. Once you have established a connection with the spirits of the ocean, focus your intention on invoking the spirit of mermaids. Visualise them emerging from the water and surrounding you, filling you with their energy and magic.

5. Mermaids are often associated with beauty, grace, and the ocean's abundance. Offer them a gift that reflects these qualities, such as fresh flowers, a piece of jewellery, or a seashell.

6. Clearly express your intention for why you are invoking the spirit of mermaids. This might include seeking their guidance, tapping into their power, or simply connecting with their energy.

7. Once you have made your offering and expressed your intention, thank the mermaids for their presence and close the ritual by blowing out any candles or other sources of flame.

By performing this ritual, you can invoke the spirit of merfolk to assist you with your magical work. Whether you are seeking their guidance, tapping into their power, or simply exploring their world of, this ritual can help you achieve your desire.

III. Using Mermaid Energy in Witchcraft

A. Enhancing Spell Work with Mermaid Energy

Mermaid energy can be a powerful addition to your spell work, enhancing the potency of your spells and helping you tap into the magic of the great ocean. Here are a few ways to incorporate mermaid energy into your spell work:

Use ocean-themed objects: Incorporate ocean-themed objects into your spell work to amplify the mermaid energy you are calling upon. This might include using seashells, ocean-themed candles, or mermaid figurines. Make these more personal by adding something handmade as the merfolk will greatly appreciate the extra effort.

Perform spells near bodies of water: Performing spells near bodies of water, such as oceans, lakes, or rivers, can enhance a spell's power by drawing upon the energy of the water.

Utilise water-based magic: Incorporate water-based magic into your spell work, such as using a ritual bath or shower, or casting spells with water.

Incorporate mermaid-themed affirmations: Affirmations are a powerful tool for directing your intention and enhancing spell work. Use mermaid-themed affirmations to focus your intention and tap into the power of merfolk.

Visualise yourself as a mermaid: Visualise yourself as a mermaid while performing spells, imagining yourself with the power and grace of these mythical creatures.

By incorporating these techniques into your work, you can enhance the potency of your spells and tap into the magic of their magical spirit.

B. Mermaid Magic for Healing and Protection

Mermaid magic can be a powerful tool for healing and protection, drawing upon the strength and beauty of these creatures to enhance your well-being and keep you safe. Here are a few ways to incorporate mermaid magic into your healing and protection practice:

Perform a mermaid healing ritual: Create a ritual that focuses on mermaid magic for healing. This might include a ritual bath, visualisation exercises, or affirmations.

Use ocean-themed crystals: Incorporate ocean-themed crystals into your healing practice, such as aquamarine, sea glass, or moonstone. These crystals can help amplify the restorative power of mermaid magic.

Visualise mermaids surrounding you: Visualise mermaids surrounding you and filling you with their spirit and magic, providing protection and promoting healing.

Create a mermaid talisman: Create a mermaid talisman to carry with you, such as a seashell, a mermaid figurine, or a piece of jewellery. This can serve as a constant reminder of the power of mermaid magic and provide you with protection throughout the day.

Use affirmations: Affirmations are a powerful tool for directing your intention and enhancing healing and protection. Use affirmations that focus on the power of mermaids to promote healing and protection.

Allow the essence of the merfolk to fill your life and protect you on your journey. They will become a guardian, healing and restoring your energies when they are depleted, and prove an ally in times of hardship in your life.

C. Mermaids and Divination

Mermaids can also play a role in divination and can provide insights and guidance in your spiritual practice. Here are a few ways to incorporate mermaid magic into your divination practice:

Use a mermaid oracle deck: An oracle deck is a set of cards used for divination. Consider using a mermaid oracle deck to tap into the energy of mermaids and receive guidance and insights. Why not have a go a creating your own desk with your handmade drawings or paintings?

Scry with a mermaid-themed crystal: Scrying is a divination technique that involves gazing into a crystal or other reflective surface to receive messages or insights. Consider using a mermaid-themed crystal, such as aquamarine or sea glass, for scrying.

Incorporate ocean-themed symbols: Incorporate ocean-themed symbols, such as seashells, starfish, or seahorses, into your divination practice. These symbols can help you tap into the energy of mermaids and receive guidance and insights.

Use mermaid-themed tarot cards: Much like oracle cards, tarot cards can be a powerful tool for divination. Consider working with mermaid-themed tarot cards to tap into the energy of mermaids and receive guidance and insights.

Visualise mermaids providing guidance: Visualise mermaids providing guidance and insights during your divination practice, imagining them communicating messages to you through the power of the ocean.

Divination is an amazing tool to add to your craft and will allow you the opportunity to communicate directly with their source of power, enhancing your craft for the better.

IV. Mermaids and Spiritual Practice

A. Mermaid Meditation Techniques

Meditation is a powerful tool for connecting with the energy of mermaids and incorporating their magic into your spiritual practice. Here are a few mermaid meditation techniques to help you tap into this energy:

- ❖ Sit or lie down in a comfortable place, close your eyes, and visualise yourself surrounded by the ocean. Imagine the sound of the waves, the scent of saltwater, and the feeling of being submerged in the cool water. Visualise mermaids swimming around you, filling you with their energy and magic.

- ❖ Visualise a mermaid swimming towards you. Imagine her tail transforming into legs as she approaches you. See her as a beautiful and powerful being, filled with wisdom and magic. Imagine her speaking to you and sharing her secrets with you.

❖ Sit or lie down in a comfortable place, close your eyes, and focus on the sound of the ocean. Imagine yourself being surrounded by the power of the ocean, and visualise mermaids swimming around you, filling you with their energy and magic.

❖ Repeat affirmations related to mermaid magic and energy. For example, you could say,

"I am connected to the power of the ocean. Mermaids are guiding me and filling me with their magic."

Repeat these affirmations as you focus on your breath and visualize yourself surrounded by the ocean.

Using these meditation techniques in your spiritual practice will enhance your magic. Whether you are seeking peace, clarity, or a deeper understanding of the mysteries of the ocean, these meditation techniques can help.

B. Mermaids and Chakra Healing

Mermaid energy can also be used to heal and balance your chakras. Here are a few ways to incorporate mermaid magic into your chakra healing practice:

Water element meditation: Focus on the water element, which is associated with the second chakra, or the sacral chakra. Imagine a waterfall cascading down your spine, washing away any blockages or negativity. Visualise mermaids swimming around you, filling you with their healing energy.

Mermaid affirmations for the sacral chakra: Repeat affirmations related to the sacral chakra and mermaid magic. For example, you could say, "I am connected to my creative and sensual energy. Mermaids are filling me with their healing energy and helping me to balance my sacral chakra."

Ocean sound therapy: Play a recording of ocean sounds or the sound of waves crashing on the shore while focusing on your sacral chakra. Imagine the sound of the ocean washing away any blockages or negativity in your sacral chakra and visualise mermaids filling you with their healing energy.

Mermaid visualisation for the sacral chakra:
Visualise a mermaid swimming towards you and placing her hands on your sacral chakra. See her filling your sacral chakra with her healing energy and light, and imagine the chakra becoming balanced and energised.

C. Mermaids and Energy Work

Mermaid energy can also be used to heal and balance your chakras. Here are a few ways to incorporate mermaid magic into your chakra healing practice:

Water element meditation: Focus on the water element, which is associated with the second chakra, or the sacral chakra. Imagine a waterfall cascading down your spine, washing away any blockages or negativity. Visualize mermaids swimming around you, filling you with their healing energy.

Mermaid affirmations for the sacral chakra: Repeat affirmations related to the sacral chakra and mermaid magic. For example, you could say,

"I am connected to my creative and sensual energy. Mermaids are filling me with their healing energy and helping me to balance my sacral chakra."

Ocean sound therapy: Play a recording of ocean sounds or the sound of waves crashing on the shore while focusing on your sacral chakra.

Imagine the sound of the ocean washing away any blockages or negativity in your sacral chakra and visualise mermaids filling you with their healing energy.

Mermaid visualisation for the sacral chakra: Visualise a mermaid swimming towards you and placing her hands on your sacral chakra. See her filling your sacral chakra with her healing energy and light and imagine the chakra becoming balanced and energised.

Incorporating these techniques into your chakra healing practice will allow you can tap into the power of the merfolk and use their energy to heal and balance your chakras. You may be seeking to heal a specific issue and these steps can help you achieve your goals.

V. Advanced Techniques

A. Mermaids and Dream Magic

Keeping a mermaid dream journal is an excellent way to connect with the energy of these mythical creatures and unlock their magic in your life. Dreams can be a powerful source of guidance, inspiration, and healing, and by focusing on the themes and symbols related to mermaids, you can tap into their power and receive messages from your subconscious mind.

To start your mermaid dream journal, you'll need a notebook and a pen that you feel comfortable using. You can decorate your journal with pictures or images of mermaids that inspire you, or write affirmations and quotes related to the magic of mermaids. Before you go to bed, take some time to meditate, visualise, or perform a ritual to connect with the energy of mermaids and invite them into your dreams.

When you wake up in the morning, spend some time writing down your dreams in as much detail as possible. Pay attention to the emotions, symbols, and messages that you received in your dreams, and reflect on how they relate to your life and your spiritual practice. You may also want to keep a record of any dreams that have a particularly strong connection to the world of mermaids or that feature mermaids as prominent characters.

In addition to recording your dreams, you can also use your mermaid dream journal to write about your experiences with mermaid magic, including any spells, meditations, or rituals that you have performed. You can also include any insights or epiphanies that you have had or use your journal as a place to reflect on your goals and aspirations and how you can use the power of merfolk to help you achieve them.

By keeping a mermaid dream journal, you can deepen your connection to the magic of these beings and unlock their power in your life. Whether you're looking for guidance, inspiration, or just a deeper understanding of yourself, this journal is a powerful tool that will help you tap into the power of mermaids and unleash your inner magic.

B. Mermaids and Elemental Magic

Working with the essence of mermaids can greatly enhance your powers of elemental magic. As you know they are connected to the element of water, which represents emotions, intuition, and the unconscious mind. By using the spirit of mermaids, you can channel this energy and work with it to amplify your abilities to manipulate and work with the elements.

For example, if you are performing a spell or ritual that involves calling upon the element of water for purification or healing, incorporating the energy of merfolk can help to magnify its potency. You can visualise the spirit helping you to direct the flow of the water element, purifying your energy and empowering your intention.

Mermaids are also associated with the moon, which is linked to the tides of the ocean and the ebb and flow of emotions. This connection makes mermaids ideal for working with spells and rituals related to the phases of the moon. You can call upon the mermaid spirit to help you to harness the power of the moon and direct it towards your manifestation goals.

Working with the energy of mermaids can also enhance your ability to control your workings with the elements of air and earth, as mermaids are associated with the ocean and its surrounding landscape. By connecting with the spirit of mermaids, you can focus the energy of the ocean's wind and waves and the earth's rock formations and plants, ramping up your powers of manifestation and allowing you to work more effectively with the elements.

C. Working with Mermaids for Manifestation

  Mermaids can play a key role in boosting your manifestation powers, and help you bring your desires to reality. There are several ways that mermaid energy can support and enhance your manifestation practices.

Their energy is often associated with emotional balance and stability, which can help you stay focused and centred as you work towards your goals. When you're feeling balanced and calm, you're better able to tap into your manifestation power and bring your desires to fruition.

Mermaids are often seen as symbols of creativity and intuition, and their energy can help you tap into your own inner wisdom and imagination. This can be especially helpful when it comes to manifestation, as it can help you come up with new and innovative solutions to the challenges you face. By accessing your intuition, you can also get in touch with what your soul truly desires, and gain clarity on what it is you're trying to manifest.

As they are associated with the water element, they are symbolic of emotions, intuition, and the unconscious mind. By tapping into this element, you can access your innermost desires and get in touch with the parts of yourself that may be holding you back. This can help you gain a deeper understanding of what you truly want and what may be standing in your way, allowing you to manifest with more precision and power.

Mer-energy is powerful and potent, and it can help to boost your manifestation power and increase the likelihood of your desires coming to fruition. This can be especially helpful if you're having trouble manifesting something specific, or if you're feeling blocked in some way. By invoking the energy of the mermaids, you can overcome any obstacles that may be standing in your way and bring your desires to reality more quickly and easily.

This form of spirit can also protect you from negative energies and cultivate a sense of well-being. It can help you feel more confident and capable as you work towards your goals and can assist you with overcoming any obstacles that may arise along the way. With a strong sense of protection and a clear mind, you can focus on your manifestation goals and bring your desires to reality more effectively.

Be sure to add some mer-magic into your daily life for the best results for your life.

VI. Conclusion

A. The Power of Mermaids in Your Life

Intuition and psychic abilities play an important role in many spiritual practices, and mermaids can be especially helpful in this regard.

Mermaids are associated with the unconscious mind and the emotions, making them ideal for those seeking to connect with their intuition. By working with the spirit of mermaids, you can use into this energy and access the wisdom of your unconscious mind, helping you to make better decisions and trust your instincts.

They are also believed to have strong psychic abilities themselves, and working with their energy can help to enhance your own psychic abilities. This can include clairvoyance, clairaudience, and other forms of intuitive perception.

As we know they are associated with the ocean and the flow of water, and this serves to remind us to let go of control and trust our instincts. By connecting with their spirit, you can learn to trust your instincts more fully and make decisions based on your intuition, rather than relying solely on logic and reason.

Merfolk are also aligned with dream magic and the realm of the subconscious mind. By keeping a mermaid dream journal and working with them, you can use your dreams to enhance your intuition and psychic abilities.

Overall, working with the mermaids can be a powerful way to enhance your psychic practices. Choosing to work with mermaid magic into your life can help you to access the guidance of your unconscious mind and trust your instincts more fully.

B. Maintaining a Connection with Mermaids

There are many reasons why one might choose to stay connected to the spirit of mermaids. Let's recap on the elements we have discovered in this book:

Emotional healing: Mermaids are associated with the emotions and the unconscious mind, making them ideal for those seeking emotional healing. By connecting with the spirit of mermaids, you can access the wisdom of your unconscious mind and release any emotional blocks that may be holding you back.

Enhancing intuition: Merfolk are also associated with intuition and psychic abilities, making them ideal for those seeking to enhance their intuition and tap into their inner wisdom.

Dream magic: Mermaids can be found within the realm of the subconscious mind and are especially poignant in dream magic, making them ideal for those seeking to work with their dreams and enhance their intuition.

Elemental magic: Mermaids are known for the element of water, making them ideal for those seeking to work with the elements and tap into the power of nature.

Healing and protection: Merfolk are synonymous with healing and protection, making them ideal for those seeking to enhance their physical and emotional well-being.

Enhancing manifestation: Mermaids can also assist with manifestation and the power of the unconscious mind, making them ideal for those seeking to bring their desires into reality.

Overall, there are many reasons why you might choose to stay connected to the spirit of mermaids, bringing more peace, healing, and abundance into your life. . The power of mermaids can bring joy, love, and magic to you, so don't be afraid to embrace them and make working with them a part of your daily routine.

C. Final Thoughts on Mermaid Magic

In conclusion, the power of mermaids is a powerful and transformative force that can enhance your spiritual practice, your spell work, and your daily life.

By connecting with mermaid energy and incorporating mer-magic into your routine, you can tap into the wisdom, power, and magic of the ocean and its inhabitants.

Whether you are seeking to heal yourself or others, protect from darkness, or manifest your true desires or intensions, the power of merfolk can help you achieve your wishes.

So, dive into the world of mermaid magic and embrace them in your life.

Remember to always approach your spiritual practice with an open heart and mind and be willing to explore new and exciting paths on your journey towards enlightenment.

VII. References and Further Reading

A. Books and Websites for Further Study

For those interested in further studying the power of mermaids and incorporating their energy into their spiritual practice, there are several books and websites that can provide valuable insights and information.

Here are a few resources to consider:

Books:

1. "Mermaid Magic: Working with the Energy of the Ocean" by Doreen Virtue

2. "The Sea Witch's Guide to Mermaid Magic" by Lucy Cavendish

3. "The Complete Book of Mermaids" by Cassandra Eason

4. "Enchantments of the Sea: Mermaid Magic for Women" by S.L. Ophelia

Websites:

1. mermaidwisdom.com

2. mermaidmagic.org

3. sea-witch.com

4. mermaidsspirit.com

These resources can provide a wealth of information on mermaid magic and energy work, as well as offer tips and techniques for use mermaid magic into your work. Never stop working on your connection with the power of the ocean and its inhabitant as it will bring fulfilment and success to you in all you choose to pursue.

B. Recommended Mermaid Spells and Rituals.

Here are a few examples of mermaid spells and rituals. Feel free to make alterations to make them truly unique to your intensions:

Mermaid Protection Spell:

❖ Fill a blue or green glass jar with salt water and add a few drops of lavender oil.

❖ Close the jar and hold it in your hands, visualizing yourself surrounded by a protective bubble of mermaid energy.

❖ Repeat the following words:

"Mermaids of the ocean, surround me with your love and protection. Keep me safe and secure, in this world and the next. So be it."

❖ Leave the jar in a place where you can see it often and renew the spell whenever you feel the need for extra protection.

Mermaid Healing Spell:

❖ Fill a bathtub with warm salt water and add a few drops of eucalyptus oil.

❖ Light a white candle and place it near the tub. Sit in the water and close your eyes, visualizing yourself surrounded by the healing energy of the mermaids.

❖ Repeat the following words:

"Mermaids of the ocean, heal my body and my soul. Wash away my pain and restore me to health. So be it."

❖ Stay in the bath for as long as you like and allow the mermaid energy to work its magic.

Mermaid Manifestation Spell:

❖ Write down your manifestation goal on a piece of paper and place it in a blue or green glass jar.

❖ Fill the jar with salt water and add a few small seashells.

❖ Close the jar and hold it in your hands, visualizing your goal becoming a reality.

❖ Repeat the following words:

"Mermaids of the ocean, bring my manifestation to me. Make my dreams come true, with your power and your magic. So be it."

❖ Leave the jar in a place where you can see it often and renew the spell whenever you feel the need for extra manifestation power.

About The Author

Astrid Ebonywood is an avid student and practitioner of the craft and has been honing her skills for many years. She has a deep passion for helping others connect with their inner magic and harness the power of spirituality and witchcraft to improve their lives.

Having developed her gifts early, Astrid devotes her time and energy to enhancing the lives of others through her teachings.

And after many years of research, experience and a gaining a vast amount of knowledge, Astrid has now fulfilled a lifelong dream of becoming a writer. Allowing her teachings to branch out across the world, promoting her message of positivity, hope and love to all.

Astrid resides in the UK with her devoted Husband and has been blessed with her beautiful children.

If You Enjoyed
This Book

Please consider leaving a review on Amazon!

As a self-employed, self-publishing creative, reviews are essential to get my content out for more people to enjoy.

Your review can make a huge difference!

Thank you for being here until the end, and keep your eyes peeled for my …

NEW BOOKS COMING SOON!

Join my Facebook Page to stay connected: -

Search 'Astrid Ebonywood – Author'

https://www.facebook.com/profile.php?id=1000898 53896988

Printed in Great Britain
by Amazon

23825591R00030